JEFFREY GUNTLY

Anatomy of a Sentence

Bridging AI and English Grammar

JX

First published by JX Stories and Media 2024

This book incorporates content generated with the assistance of Artificial Intelligence (AI), specifically leveraging OpenAI's ChatGPT. The AI has been utilized for generating insights, enhancing explanations, and providing examples related to the book's focus on the intersection of English grammar and AI technology. The author has reviewed, edited, and curated the AI-generated content to ensure accuracy, relevance, and coherence with the book's educational objectives.

First edition

ISBN: 978-0-9852453-9-9

This book was professionally typeset on Reedsy.
Find out more at reedsy.com

To Garrett, who always believes I'm smarter than I am

Contents

1

Introduction

In an era increasingly defined by the intersection of technology and daily life, artificial intelligence (AI) has emerged as a powerful force reshaping the very fabric of communication. My journey into the fusion of linguistic tradition and AI innovation began not in a laboratory or a tech company, but in the quiet corners of a personal project that sought to harness the capabilities of ChatGPT, a leading AI language model. This book, "Anatomy of a Sentence: Bridging AI and English Grammar," unfolds from my exploration into the fascinating parallels and divergences between human understanding of language and AI's computational interpretations.

Rooted in the nuances of the English language, this exploration is as much about the structure of sentences and grammar as it is about the unforeseen boundaries and possibilities of AI. My singular focus on English stems from both my expertise and the practical necessity of delving deep into one language's intricacies, offering readers a detailed examination that intertwines the rich traditions of English grammar with the cutting-edge precision of AI technology.

The spark for this venture ignited during an experiment with ChatGPT aimed at simplifying complex legal jargon into plain language. As I input sentences laden with technicalities, expecting AI to demystify the legalese, I encountered a surprising challenge: the AI persistently misinterpreted the context, offering explanations that, while technically accurate, missed the essence of the legal concepts. This experience highlighted a pivotal realization—the gap between AI's remarkable linguistic capabilities and its grasp of human context and nuance. It was a moment of clarity that illustrated not just the limitations of AI, but also its potential as a tool for enhancing our understanding and use of language, provided we navigate its capabilities with insight and creativity.

Thus began the journey chronicled in this book, one that weaves through the anatomy of sentences to uncover how AI can both mirror our linguistic processes and chart its own unique path through language. This exploration is not confined to the academic; it is a narrative shaped by firsthand experiences with AI, an invitation to readers to traverse the bridge between the art of language and the science of algorithms.

By focusing on the English language, this book aims to offer a lens through which readers can gain insightful perspectives on the interaction between human communication skills and technological advancements. It is a testament to the collaborative power that lies at the intersection of human ingenuity and artificial intelligence—a partnership that holds the promise of transforming our approach to language and communication.

Together, we delve not only into the mechanics of language but also into the expansive possibilities that arise when we view AI as a collaborator in our linguistic explorations. This book is both a guide and a companion on a journey to understanding the complex dance between the structure of language and the algorithms that seek to decode it, paving the way for a future where technology and language coalesce to enrich our communication and creativity.

2

Understanding Sentence Structure

In the "Understanding Sentence Structure" section, we'll explore how sentences, the core units of language, function. Beyond simple word chains, sentences are intricate structures where each word and phrase have its role, ensuring our messages are conveyed precisely. We'll break down the roles of subjects, verbs, and objects, and delve into modifiers and clauses that add depth and clarity to our expressions.

This exploration serves a dual purpose: to refine our grasp of English sentence structure and to shed light on how AI interprets our language. By marrying traditional grammar with insights into AI's linguistic processing, we aim to foster a deeper appreciation for the craft of sentence construction.

Designed for readers across the spectrum, from language enthusiasts to those curious about AI's role in language understanding, this section promises to enrich your communication skills through a concise yet comprehensive examination of sentence architecture. Join us to discover the elegance and complexity of sentence structure, an essential skill in both human expression and technological innovation.

The Parts of Speech

The English language is composed of eight primary parts of speech. Each plays a unique role in sentence construction, allowing for the expression of actions, descriptions, relationships, and emotions.

Nouns

Nouns are words that name people, places, things, or ideas. They serve as the subjects or objects within a sentence.

- **Proper Nouns**: Name specific people, places, or organizations (e.g., "London," "Elizabeth").
- **Common Nouns**: Name general items or concepts (e.g., "city," "woman").
- **Concrete Nouns**: Name physical objects (e.g., "book," "chair").
- **Abstract Nouns**: Name ideas, qualities, or states (e.g., "freedom," "love").

Verbs

Verbs express actions or states of being. They are central to the predicate of a sentence, indicating what the subject is doing or being.

- **Action Verbs**: Show physical or mental actions (e.g., "run," "think").
- **Linking Verbs**: Connect the subject to a subject complement that describes or identifies it (e.g., "am," "seem").

- **Auxiliary Verbs**: Help the main verb express tense, mood, or voice (e.g., "has," "will").

Adjectives

Adjectives describe or modify nouns and pronouns, providing details that enhance understanding.

- **Descriptive Adjectives**: Qualify nouns directly (e.g., "red," "tall").
- **Quantitative Adjectives**: Indicate quantity or amount (e.g., "several," "many").
- **Demonstrative Adjectives**: Point out specific items (e.g., "this," "those").

Adverbs

Adverbs modify verbs, adjectives, or other adverbs, offering information about how, when, where, why, or to what extent an action is performed.

- **Manner Adverbs**: Describe how an action is performed (e.g., "slowly," "quietly").
- **Time Adverbs**: Indicate when an action happens (e.g., "yesterday," "soon").
- **Place Adverbs**: Show where an action occurs (e.g., "here," "everywhere").

Pronouns

Pronouns replace nouns to avoid repetition and simplify sentences. They must agree in number and gender with the nouns they replace.

- **Personal Pronouns**: Refer to specific persons or things (e.g., "he," "they").
- **Possessive Pronouns**: Indicate ownership (e.g., "hers," "ours").
- **Relative Pronouns**: Introduce relative clauses (e.g., "who," "which").

Prepositions

Prepositions show the relationship between a noun (or pronoun) and other words in a sentence, often indicating location, direction, or time.

- Examples: "in," "at," "on," "between," "during."

Conjunctions

Conjunctions join words, phrases, or clauses, indicating their relationship to each other.

- **Coordinating Conjunctions**: Connect grammatically equal elements (e.g., "and" "but").
- **Subordinating Conjunctions**: Introduce dependent clauses (e.g., "although," "because").

Interjections

Interjections are words or phrases that express emotion or exclamation, often standing apart from the main sentence structure.

- Examples: "Wow!," "Oh," "Alas."

Understanding the structure of sentences is pivotal in both generating clear communication and comprehending the nuances of the English language. Traditional grammar categorizes the elements of sentences into several key components, each playing a vital role in conveying meaning effectively.

8 PARTS OF SPEECH
1
NOUNS
Nouns identify everything in our world, acting as the backbone of sentences by naming people, places, things, or ideas. They're essential for giving our sentences subjects to discuss and objects to interact with, making them foundational to the structure and meaning of our communication.
2
VERBS
Verbs depict actions or states, driving the narrative of a sentence. They are central to expressing what's happening, making them indispensable for adding dynamism and intention to our language.
3
ADJECTIVES
Adjectives provide detail and richness to nouns, allowing for precise and vivid descriptions. Their role is key in painting a vivid picture in the listener's or reader's mind, enhancing the expressive power of language.
4
ADVERBS
Adverbs modify verbs, adjectives, or other adverbs, offering nuanced details about actions or qualities. They enrich sentences by providing context on how, when, where, and to what extent actions occur, making our descriptions more comprehensive.
5
PRONOUNS
Pronouns replace nouns to avoid repetition, making our language more efficient and less cumbersome. They are crucial for maintaining clarity and coherence in discourse, especially in complex narratives or discussions.
6
PREPOSITIONS
Prepositions link nouns or pronouns to other words, establishing relationships of time, space, and logic. They are vital for constructing complex, interconnected thoughts that reflect the intricacies of our experiences.
7
CONJUCTIONS
Conjunctions join words, phrases, or clauses, ensuring flow and coherence. They play a critical role in building complex ideas and maintaining the logical progression of thoughts, crucial for effective communication.
8
INTERJECTIONS
Interjections express spontaneous emotions or reactions, adding immediacy and emotional depth to language. They serve as powerful tools for conveying surprise, delight, or other strong feelings, enriching our interactions with a human touch.

Infographic 1, depicting the importance of each part of speech.

The Parts of a Sentence

Subjects, Predicates, and Objects

Subject: The subject of a sentence is the person, place, thing, or idea that is performing the action or being described. It's what or whom the sentence is about.

- *Example*: In the sentence "The quick brown fox jumps over the lazy dog," the quick brown fox is the subject.

Predicate: The predicate contains the verb and tells something about the subject. It explains what the subject does or is like.

- *Example*: In the same sentence, *jumps over the lazy dog* is the predicate, describing the action of the subject.

Object: The object receives the action of the verb. Objects are either direct (receiving the action directly) or indirect (receiving the action indirectly).

- *Example*: In "She gave her friend a gift," *a gift* is the direct object, and *her friend* is the indirect object.

Modifiers: Adjectives and Adverbs

Modifiers provide additional information about the subjects, objects, or verbs they describe, specifying "how," "when," "where," and "to what extent" something happened.

Adjectives modify nouns and pronouns, adding detail or description.

- *Example*: In "The *loud* noise startled me," *loud* is an adjective modifying *noise*.

Adverbs modify verbs, adjectives, or other adverbs, often ending in -ly.

- *Example*: In "He ran *quickly*," *quickly* is an adverb modifying the verb *ran*.

Clause Types: Independent and Dependent

Independent Clauses can stand alone as a sentence. They have a subject and a predicate and express a complete thought.

- *Example*: "The sun set."

Dependent Clauses cannot stand alone as a sentence. They also contain a subject and a predicate but require an independent clause to form a complete sentence.

- *Example*: "When the sun set" is a dependent clause that needs to be joined with an independent clause, like "we went home," to make a complete sentence: "When the sun set, we went home."

Understanding these fundamental elements and how they interact within a sentence provides a solid foundation for both analyzing sentence structure and crafting effective sentences. This knowledge is crucial not only in traditional grammar but also in understanding the nuances of how AI interprets and generates language.

Understanding Sentence Structure: Types of Sentences

In English, understanding how sentences are structured is fundamental to both expressing ideas clearly and grasping the nuances of language. This section will delve into the four main types of sentence structures: simple, compound, complex, and compound-complex. Each type plays a unique role in communication, offering varying degrees of complexity and nuance.

Simple Sentences

A simple sentence consists of a single independent clause. It has a subject and a predicate and expresses a complete thought.

- **Example**: "The technology advances rapidly."
- **AI Interpretation**: AI models recognize simple sentences easily, processing them efficiently due to their straightforward structure. These sentences are often used by AI for clear and concise responses.

Compound Sentences

Compound sentences contain two or more independent clauses joined by a coordinating conjunction (for, and, nor, but, or, yet, so) or a semicolon. Each clause in a compound sentence could stand alone as a simple sentence.

- **Example**: "The software was updated, but the system still crashed."
- **AI Interpretation**: AI can distinguish the individual clauses within compound sentences and understand their relationship, based on the conjunctions used. This allows for responses that consider the entirety of the compound structure.

Complex Sentences

Complex sentences are composed of one independent clause and one or more dependent clauses connected by subordinating conjunctions (because, since, after, although, etc.). These sentences convey a deeper level of relation between ideas.

- **Example**: "Although the AI passed the test, it cannot think independently."
- **AI Interpretation**: AI analyzes complex sentences by identifying the main clause and the subordinate clause, understanding the dependency between them. This is crucial for interpreting the context and nuances of requests or statements.

Compound-Complex Sentences

Compound-complex sentences combine the elements of compound and complex sentences. They contain two or more independent clauses and one or more dependent clauses.

- **Example**: "The robot corrected its course when it encountered an obstacle, and it reached its destination on time."
- **AI Interpretation**: Processing compound-complex sentences is more challenging for AI due to their intricacy. AI must analyze the sentence in parts, understanding both the relationships between independent clauses and the role of dependent clauses.

Practical Implications

These sentence types form the basis of English communication, enabling us to articulate thoughts with varying degrees of complexity and subtlety. For AI, understanding these structures is key to interpreting human language accurately and responding appropriately. As we interact with AI, being mindful of these sentence types can help us craft prompts that are easier for AI to understand and respond to, enhancing our communication with technology.

Through exploring these sentence structures, we gain insight into the versatility and depth of the English language. This knowledge is not only essential for effective communication but also enriches our engagement with AI, offering a glimpse into how technology interprets and processes our language.

Activity: Crafting and Refining Sentences with AI

Part 1

Objective

Engage with the intricacies of the English language by constructing complex sentences that reflect real-world scenarios or thoughts. This exercise encourages critical thinking, creativity, and the practical application of grammar, appealing to the adult learner's experiences and intellectual interests.

Instructions

1. Theme Selection: Choose a theme that resonates with your experiences or interests. This could be technology, current events, personal growth, or professional development.
2. Word Bank Creation: Create a word bank relevant to your selected theme, including: **Nouns**: Identify 3-5 nouns that are central to your theme; **Verbs**: Select 3-5 verbs that vividly describe actions or states related to your nouns; **Adjectives**: Pick 2-4 adjectives to provide depth and description to your nouns; **Adverbs**: Choose 1-3 adverbs to modify your verbs, adding nuance to the actions or states.
3. Sentence Construction: Using your word bank, construct a complex sentence that incorporates an independent clause and at least one dependent clause. Aim to use a variety of parts of speech to create a sentence that is both grammatically complex and meaningful.

Example for the theme "Technology": "As the digital landscape continues to evolve, professionals who adapt quickly, leveraging new tools and platforms, find themselves at the forefront of innovation."

Analysis and Reflection:

Analyze: Break down your sentence by labeling each word with its corresponding part of speech. Reflect on how each element contributes to the overall meaning of the sentence.

Reflect: Consider how constructing this sentence has deepened your understanding of sentence structure and the parts of speech. How does this exercise relate to your real-world communication, whether in writing or speech?

Part 2

Objective

In this part of the activity, you'll work with ChatGPT to refine and expand the complex sentence you've created. The goal is to explore how AI can contribute to the art of sentence construction, offering insights that can further enhance clarity, depth, and engagement.

Instructions

1. Input Your Sentence: Start by inputting your constructed sentence into ChatGPT. Briefly explain the context or theme of the sentence to give ChatGPT a clear starting point.

2. Request Enhancements: Ask ChatGPT to enhance your sentence by:

- Improving clarity and readability without losing complexity.
- Adding stylistic elements to make the sentence more engaging or persuasive.
- Suggesting alternative words or phrases that could add nuance or precision.

Analysis and Reflection

Analyze: Judge the enhanced sentence's clarity and its effectiveness in conveying the intended message. Evaluate the impact of stylistic enhancements or precise language on engagement. Lastly, assess the sentence's fidelity to the original theme and intent, and the AI's ability to preserve your core message.

Reflect: Reflect on how collaborating with ChatGPT affected your perception of sentence construction. Consider aspects like:

- The benefits of using AI as a tool for refining language.
- Limitations you noticed in AI's suggestions or understanding.
- Potential applications of AI in your writing or professional communication tasks.

Bonus Activity:

Feedback Loop: Optionally, you can iterate on this process by providing feedback to ChatGPT based on your analysis and seeing how it adjusts its suggestions. This step can offer insights into the adaptability of AI in refining language based on human input.

Conclusion

As we conclude our exploration of "Understanding Sentence Structure," we stand on the precipice of an exciting continuation of our journey: delving into how AI interprets a sentence. This forthcoming section promises to deepen our appreciation of the complexities and capabilities of language processing through the lens of artificial intelligence. Our journey through traditional grammar has laid a solid foundation, equipping us with the knowledge to not only understand but also critically engage with AI's linguistic methodologies.

The upcoming exploration into AI's interpretation of sentences will not only illuminate the technical processes behind language models like ChatGPT but also offer insights into the parallels and divergences between human and machine understanding of language. By bridging the gap between the grammatical principles discussed and the computational algorithms employed by AI, we'll uncover the nuances of how AI comprehends, generates, and refines language.

This transition from the structures of traditional grammar to the realms of AI interpretation represents a fascinating melding of worlds. It invites us to consider the implications of AI's growing role in our daily communications and creative expressions. As we embark on this next phase, our grounding in sentence structure will serve as a critical lens through which to appreciate and critique the evolving capabilities of AI in understanding and utilizing the English language.

In essence, the journey ahead is not just about observing

AI's approach to language; it's about engaging with the future of communication itself. As we move into examining how AI interprets a sentence, we carry forward the insights and questions sparked by our grammatical explorations, poised to navigate the intersections of linguistics and technology with informed curiosity and critical thought.

3

AI's Interpretation of Sentences

Part-of-Speech Tagging

As we venture into the new section focused on how AI interprets a sentence, we delve deeper into the sophisticated mechanisms that enable machines to process and understand human language. A pivotal aspect of this journey is exploring the role of Part-of-Speech (POS) tagging, a fundamental step in the realm of Natural Language Processing (NLP) that acts as a critical intermediary between mere strings of text and the rich, structured information they convey.

POS tagging is more than just a preliminary task; it's the linchpin that allows AI to decipher the syntactic skeleton of sentences. By meticulously categorizing each word into its appropriate grammatical role — whether it be a noun, verb, adjective, and so forth — based on both its inherent meaning and the context it's used within, AI can begin to parse the underlying structure of language. This process is instrumental in enabling AI to grasp the multifaceted relationships between words, an understanding that is essential for accurately interpreting sentences and extracting their meaning.

This understanding lays the foundation for more advanced NLP tasks such as syntactic parsing, semantic analysis, and sentiment detection, each of which builds upon the initial insights provided by POS tagging. Through syntactic parsing, AI systems delve into the architecture of sentences, uncovering how words group into phrases and clauses to express complex ideas. Semantic analysis takes this a step further by interpreting the meanings and implications of those structures, enabling AI to comprehend subtleties, nuances, and the intent behind words.

Furthermore, the POS tagging process illuminates the challenges AI faces in language understanding, from dealing with homonyms and polysemes — words with multiple meanings — to navigating the intricacies of language that evolve over time. These challenges highlight the ongoing dialogue between linguistic theory and computational practice, a conversation that continually refines AI's approach to language.

In this section, we will explore the sophisticated algorithms and models that underpin POS tagging and subsequent language processing tasks, unraveling how AI systems like ChatGPT interpret, generate, and interact with human language. By examining these processes, we gain not only a deeper appreciation for the capabilities and limitations of current AI technology but also insights into the future directions of AI in enhancing our interactions with the digital world. This exploration is not just about understanding AI but about envisioning the possibilities that lie at the intersection of technology, language, and human creativity.

The Process of POS Tagging

1. **Tokenization**: Initially, the sentence is broken down into individual words or tokens. For example, the sentence "The quick brown fox jumps over the lazy dog" is divided into tokens: [The, quick, brown, fox, jumps, over, the, lazy, dog].
2. **Word Analysis**: Each token is then analyzed to determine its possible parts of speech. Many words in English can serve as more than one part of speech depending on their use in a sentence (e.g., "run" can be a verb or a noun).
3. **Contextual Understanding**: AI uses the context of each word within the sentence to decide on the most appropriate part of speech. For instance, in the sentence above, "quick" and "brown" are identified as adjectives modifying "fox," a noun, based on their position and usage.
4. **Application of Rules and Machine Learning Models**: AI systems apply grammatical rules and patterns learned from training data to accurately tag each word. Advanced systems utilize machine learning models, particularly those based on neural networks, which have been trained on large corpora of text annotated with correct POS tags.
5. **Handling Ambiguity**: AI uses statistical probabilities to resolve ambiguities, choosing the most likely part of speech based on the word's usage across the training data. For example, if "run" appears after "a," the AI is likely to tag it as a noun because of the common pattern of an article followed by a noun.

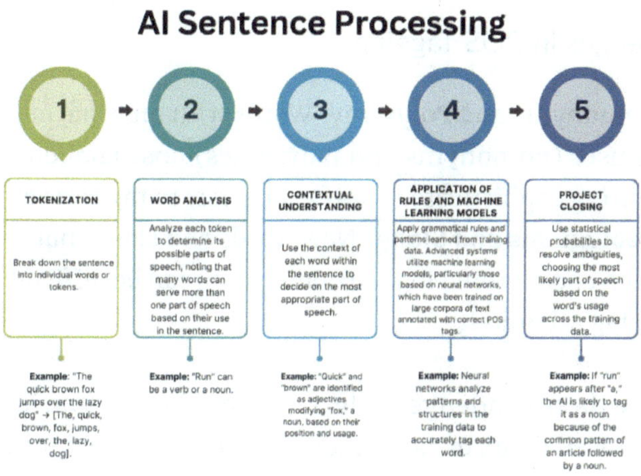

Chart 1, depicting the 5 steps of AI sentence processing

Importance of POS Tagging in AI

- **Foundation for Further Analysis**: POS tagging is foundational for syntactic and semantic analysis, enabling AI to parse sentences more accurately and understand complex structures.
- **Improves Machine Translation**: Knowing the parts of speech helps AI translate languages more accurately, as it can better maintain the grammatical structure of sentences.
- **Enables Query Understanding**: For search engines and virtual assistants, POS tagging helps in understanding the intent behind user queries, distinguishing between nouns (subjects of interest) and verbs (actions) to provide relevant

responses.

Challenges in POS Tagging

- **Homonyms and Polysemy**: Words with multiple meanings or uses (homonyms and polysemes) pose challenges, requiring sophisticated context analysis to tag correctly.
- **Neologisms and Slang**: New words and slang that haven't been encountered in the training data can be difficult for AI to tag accurately.

Despite these challenges, advancements in machine learning and the availability of vast annotated datasets have significantly improved the accuracy of POS tagging in AI systems. This step is indispensable in the journey from basic text processing to truly understanding and generating human-like language responses.

Syntactic Parsing

Syntactic parsing is an advanced stage in the language understanding process where AI examines the grammatical structure of a sentence. This involves determining how the individual words (tokens) and phrases within a sentence relate to each other to form a coherent whole. By parsing a sentence syntactically, AI systems can identify the underlying structure, which is critical for tasks such as translation, question answering, and natural language generation.

How AI Performs Syntactic Parsing

1. **Building on POS Tagging**: After each word in a sentence has been tagged with its part of speech, syntactic parsing begins. This foundational step ensures that the AI understands the basic role of each word or token.
2. **Dependency Parsing vs. Constituency Parsing**: There are two primary methods AI uses for syntactic parsing: **Dependency Parsing**: This method focuses on the dependencies between words, establishing a direct link between 'head' words and words that modify or complement them ('dependents'). For instance, in "The cat sat on the mat," dependency parsing identifies "sat" as the central verb, with "the cat" as the subject and "on the mat" as the prepositional phrase indicating location. **Constituency Parsing**: Also known as phrase-structure parsing, this approach breaks down the sentence into sub-phrases or constituents according to a set of rules (often based on context-free grammar). The result is a parse tree that shows how the sentence can be divided into smaller parts, like noun phrases (NP) or verb phrases (VP), and how these parts combine to form the complete sentence.
3. **Utilizing Parse Trees**: Regardless of the method, the goal is to construct a parse tree or a similar structural representation that illustrates the hierarchical relationships between different parts of the sentence. These trees are essential for AI to "visualize" the sentence's structure.
4. **Understanding Sentence Roles**: Through syntactic parsing, AI determines not just the function of individual words, but also higher-level sentence roles, such as subjects, predicates, and objects. This understanding allows AI to

process complex sentences with multiple clauses or nested structures.

5. **Leveraging Machine Learning**: Modern AI systems often employ machine learning models, especially those based on deep learning, to improve parsing accuracy. These models are trained on large corpora of text with annotated syntactic structures, learning to predict the most likely structure for unseen sentences.

Importance of Syntactic Parsing in AI

- **Enhancing Language Understanding**: By unraveling the grammatical structure of sentences, AI can better comprehend the meaning and intent behind text, crucial for accurate information retrieval, summarization, and interaction in natural language interfaces.
- **Supporting Complex Tasks**: Understanding the syntactic structure is vital for translating languages while maintaining grammatical correctness, generating coherent and contextually relevant text, and accurately answering queries based on text content.

Challenges in Syntactic Parsing

- **Ambiguity and Complexity**: Sentences with ambiguous or complex structures pose significant challenges, as there may be multiple valid ways to parse them. AI systems must use contextual clues and probabilistic models to choose the most likely interpretation.
- **Adapting to Language Variability**: Natural language is highly variable and creative, with new expressions and

constructions emerging constantly. AI systems need continuous updates and training to keep up with the evolving nature of language.

Syntactic parsing represents a critical junction in AI's journey from recognizing words to grasping the full nuance of language, bridging the gap between simple text processing and deep language understanding.

Entity Recognition and Relationship Understanding

Entity recognition and relationship understanding are pivotal components of Natural Language Processing (NLP) that enable AI to extract meaningful information from text by identifying key entities—such as people, places, organizations, dates, and more—and understanding the relationships between them. This process allows AI to move beyond mere word identification towards grasping the context and nuances of language.

Entity Recognition

1. **Identifying Entities**: Entity recognition involves scanning text to identify and categorize specific pieces of information into predefined classes or categories (e.g., "New York City" as a Location, "Albert Einstein" as a Person). This step is crucial for transforming unstructured text into structured data that AI systems can more easily analyze and understand.
2. **Classification and Categorization**: Utilizing machine learning models, AI categorizes each identified entity

based on context and characteristics. For instance, in the sentence "Tesla plans to build a new factory in Austin," AI recognizes "Tesla" as an organization and "Austin" as a Location.

3. **Contextual Understanding**: Advanced NLP models, especially those using deep learning, excel at distinguishing between entities with the same name but different contexts (e.g., "Apple" the company vs. "apple" the fruit) by analyzing the surrounding text.

Relationship Understanding

1. **Detecting Relationships**: Once entities are identified, AI aims to understand the relationships between them. This involves parsing the sentence structure to determine how entities are connected, such as identifying action verbs or prepositions that link entities.
2. **Building Knowledge Graphs**: By mapping out entities and their relationships, AI can construct knowledge graphs that visually represent how different entities are related. For example, in "Barack Obama was born in Hawaii," a knowledge graph would link the entity "Barack Obama" with the entity "Hawaii" through the relationship "was born in."
3. **Understanding Sentence Semantics**: Recognizing relationships between entities is key to understanding the semantic meaning of sentences. It enables AI to answer questions, summarize texts, and extract relevant information by focusing on how entities interact within the text.

Applications of Entity and Relationship Understanding

- **Information Extraction and Retrieval**: Enables efficient extraction of relevant information from large text corpora, enhances search engines, and recommendation systems.
- **Content Summarization**: Helps in summarizing articles, reports, and documents by identifying and linking the main entities and their actions.
- **Sentiment Analysis**: By recognizing entities and their relationships, AI can more accurately determine sentiments expressed about specific products, services, or individuals.
- **Question Answering Systems**: Powers chatbots and virtual assistants to understand user queries better and provide precise answers by identifying key entities and their relations in the input text.

Challenges

- **Ambiguity and Polysemy**: Distinguishing between entities with the same name but different meanings based on context remains a challenge.
- **Complex Relationships**: Understanding complex, implicit relationships between entities, especially in longer or more complex sentences, can be difficult for AI systems.

Entity recognition and relationship understanding significantly enhance AI's ability to process and interpret natural language, providing a deeper understanding of text content and context. This capability is crucial for a wide range of applications, from enhancing user interactions with chatbots to automating insights from unstructured data.

Activity: Parts of Speech Tagging

Part 1: Manual Linguistic Analysis

Objective: Dive deep into the grammatical intricacies of a complex sentence to uncover its structure, employing your linguistic knowledge to identify key components and their functions.

Task Steps:

1. **Sentence Selection**: Choose a compelling, complex sentence from a piece of contemporary writing that catches your interest or challenges your understanding.
2. **Parts of Speech Identification**: Carefully label each word in your chosen sentence with its corresponding part of speech. This step is crucial for unraveling the sentence's grammatical structure.
3. **Structure Breakdown**: Create a detailed breakdown of the sentence's structure. Identify the main subject(s) and verb(s), highlight any direct or indirect objects, and pinpoint modifiers (adjectives, adverbs). Aim to reveal how these elements interact to convey meaning.
4. **Diagramming (Optional):** If you're familiar with sentence diagramming, sketch a diagram of your sentence. This visual representation can further clarify the relationships between sentence components.

Analysis and Reflection:

Analyze: Document any difficulties you encountered during the analysis. Were certain parts of speech or structural components challenging to identify? Assess the complexity of the sentence based on your analysis. How do the identified parts of speech and their arrangement contribute to or detract from the sentence's clarity and impact?

Reflect: Reflect on what this meticulous manual analysis has taught you about sentence construction and grammatical complexity. What new understandings or appreciations have emerged from this exercise?

Part 2: Engaging with ChatGPT

Objective: Use ChatGPT to analyze the same complex sentence and compare its AI-driven linguistic breakdown to your manual analysis, gaining insights into how AI interprets and understands sentence structure.

Task Steps:

1. **Input the Sentence**: Input the complex sentence you analyzed manually into ChatGPT. Clearly ask ChatGPT to identify the parts of speech for each word and to provide an analysis of the sentence structure.
2. **Record ChatGPT's Analysis**: Document ChatGPT's interpretation of the sentence, noting the parts of speech it identifies and its breakdown of the sentence structure.
3. **Request Further Insight (Optional):** If ChatGPT's initial

analysis is intriguing, ask follow-up questions to delve deeper into its understanding. You might inquire about the reasons behind certain grammatical categorizations or ask for clarification on parts of the analysis.

Analysis and Reflection:

Analyze: Examine how ChatGPT's analysis compares with your manual breakdown. Highlight both concurrences and discrepancies in the identification of parts of speech and the understanding of sentence structure. Evaluate the accuracy and depth of ChatGPT's linguistic analysis.

Reflect: Reflect on how engaging with ChatGPT has affected your understanding of sentence structure and grammar. Has this activity altered your perspective on the potential role of AI in language learning and linguistic analysis?

Conclusion

Having journeyed through the "AI's Interpretation of Sentences" section and engaged in a hands-on activity that illuminates both manual and AI-driven analyses of sentence structure, we arrive at a pivotal moment of reflection and anticipation. This exploration has not only deepened our understanding of how AI, particularly models like ChatGPT, navigate the complex terrain of language but also highlighted the intricate dance between human grammatical intuition and artificial computational prowess.

The activity designed to juxtapose manual linguistic analysis with ChatGPT's interpretation serves as a practical demonstration of AI's capabilities and limitations. By meticulously breaking down a sentence on our own and then observing how an AI system tackles the same task, we gain insight into the nuances of language that AI can capture — and those it might overlook. This comparison sheds light on the sophisticated algorithms driving AI's understanding of syntax and semantics, revealing a fascinating blend of accuracy and imperfection in AI's linguistic endeavors.

The reflections and analyses emerging from this activity underscore a critical realization: while AI can mimic certain aspects of human sentence interpretation, there remains an unmistakable gap filled by human insight, creativity, and the subtleties of context and emotion that AI is yet to fully grasp. This understanding is crucial as we stand on the threshold of the next section, which promises to delve deeper into comparing AI and human sentence interpretation. This forthcoming exploration aims to unravel the layers of this complex relationship further, examining how the synergy between human expertise and AI technology can enhance our engagement with language.

As we prepare to transition into this comparative analysis, we carry with us the lessons learned from our hands-on activity and the broader "AI's Interpretation of Sentences" section. The upcoming section will build upon these foundations, aiming to provide a more nuanced understanding of the interplay between AI's computational approach to language and the inherently human faculty of linguistic interpretation. By examining the points of convergence and divergence between AI and human understanding, we can appreciate the unique strengths and perspectives each brings to the table.

In conclusion, the exploration of AI's interpretation of sentences, enriched by the direct engagement of the activity, sets the stage for a deeper inquiry into the collaborative potential and challenges of integrating AI into our linguistic practices. As we move forward, let us remain curious and open-minded, ready to explore the vast possibilities that lie at the intersection of artificial intelligence and human linguistic expertise.

4

Comparative Analysis: AI vs. Traditional Grammar

Case Studies

Case Study 1: "The cat sleeps on the mat."

Parts of Speech Breakdown:

- **Determiners**: "The" before "cat" and "mat" specifies particular objects.
- **Noun**: "Cat" and "mat" are nouns, identifying the subject and the object of the preposition, respectively.
- **Verb**: "Sleeps" is a verb that describes the action performed by the subject.
- **Preposition**: "On" indicates the relationship between the verb and the noun "mat," specifying location.

Grammar Analysis:

- **Sentence Type:** Simple
- **Structure**: Subject + Verb + Prepositional Phrase
- This sentence is a straightforward example of a simple sentence structure where a subject performs an action that's described by a verb, and the action's location is further detailed by a prepositional phrase.

AI Analysis (NLP):

- **Contextual Understanding**: AI's interpretation leverages not just the identification of parts of speech but also contextual data from training to understand the sentence's real-world implications, such as recognizing typical behavior associated with the subject ("cat") and how objects like "mat" fit into these scenarios.
- **Semantic Processing & Entity Recognition**: AI identifies "The cat" as a likely 'Animal' entity and "the mat" as an object. The simple action described is understood within the context of common knowledge about cats and their behaviors.
- **Dependency Parsing**: AI constructs a dependency tree to elucidate how "sleeps" serves as the central verb with "The cat" as the actor of the action and "on the mat" providing locational context. This parsing underscores the AI's capability to map out the sentence structure dynamically, reflecting a deeper layer of understanding beyond static parts of speech identification.

Case Study 2: "Although it was raining, she decided to walk to the store."

Parts of Speech Breakdown:

- **Conjunction**: "Although" introduces a contrast or condition.
- **Pronoun**: "It" and "she" serve as subjects in their respective clauses.
- **Verbs**: "Was" (auxiliary verb for the past continuous tense), "raining" (present participle form used with "was" to form the past continuous tense), and "decided" (past tense verb indicating action).
- **Infinitive Verb**: "To walk" indicates the action she decided to perform.
- **Preposition**: "To" specifies direction towards "the store."
- **Determiner**: "The" specifies a particular store.
- **Noun**: "Store" is the object of the preposition "to," indicating the destination.

Grammar Analysis:

- **Sentence Type**: Complex
- **Structure**: Dependent Clause + Independent Clause
- The sentence presents a complex structure where a dependent clause sets a condition ("Although it was raining"), and an independent clause states the consequent action ("she decided to walk to the store"). This highlights the subject's decision-making process in the face of undesirable weather conditions.

AI Analysis (NLP):

- **Contextual Understanding**: AI interprets this sentence by recognizing the conditional nature introduced by "Although." It understands that the decision to walk to the store is made despite the condition presented in the dependent clause, highlighting its ability to process causal relationships and human decisions in specific contexts.
- **Entity Recognition & Semantic Processing**: AI categorizes "it" generally as referring to the weather condition and "the store" as a specific location. It understands "she" as a person making a decision, reflecting their ability to attribute agency and action to the correct subject.
- **Dependency Parsing**: AI's parsing highlights the contrast between the condition (raining) and the action (deciding to walk), effectively mapping out the complex sentence structure. It identifies "decided" as the main verb of the action, with "to walk to the store" further detailing the action's nature and goal. The use of "Although" signals to AI that the action takes place in spite of the circumstances described in the dependent clause.

Case Study 3: "Is the library open today?"

Parts of Speech Breakdown:

- **Verb**: "Is" operates as the auxiliary verb for forming questions.
- **Determiner**: "The" specifies which library is being dis-

cussed.

- **Noun**: "Library" serves as the subject of the question.
- **Adjective**: "Open" functions as the complement to the verb "is," describing the state being inquired about.
- **Noun as Adverbial Modifier**: "Today" modifies the verb "is" to inquire about the current day.

Grammar Analysis:

- **Sentence Type**: Interrogative
- **Structure**: Auxiliary Verb + Subject + Complement + Adverbial Modifier
- This sentence is structured as a direct question that seeks to ascertain the operational status of the library on the current day, using a standard interrogative format that places the auxiliary verb at the beginning.

AI Analysis (NLP):

- **Question Interpretation**: AI recognizes the interrogative structure, focusing on the operational status (open/close) of a specified entity ("the library") at a particular time ("today"). The model employs its trained knowledge on question patterns to predict the likely information being sought.
- **Parts of Speech Tagging**: Consistent with grammatical analysis, AI identifies the auxiliary verb, determiner, noun (subject), adjective (complement), and adverbial modifier. This tagging is foundational for understanding the question's structure and intent.
- **Temporal Context and Entity Recognition**: AI distin-

guishes "today" as a temporal marker that is critical for the query's timeframe, understanding its relevance in the context of the library's operational hours. The "library" is recognized as a public place or institution, showcasing AI's ability to categorize entities based on common knowledge and training data.

- **Semantic Processing**: The AI delves into its training to infer that questions of this nature often seek binary (yes/no) responses based on operational schedules. It utilizes its database of common queries and contexts to interpret the potential user intent behind the question.

Case Study 4: "Please turn off the lights before you leave."

Parts of Speech Breakdown:

- **Interjection**: "Please" is used here as a polite request or interjection.
- **Verb Phrase (Imperative)**: "Turn off" constitutes a phrasal verb indicating the action requested to be performed.
- **Determiner**: "The" specifies which lights are being referred to.
- **Noun**: "Lights" is the direct object of the verb phrase, the items to be acted upon.
- **Conjunction**: "Before" introduces a condition or time for the action.
- **Pronoun**: "You" is the implied subject of the imperative verb, typically omitted in imperative sentences but understood as the listener.
- **Verb**: "Leave" indicates the action that "you" (the listener) is expected to perform before acting on the imperative verb

phrase.

Grammar Analysis:

- **Sentence Type**: Imperative with a temporal clause.
- **Structure**: Imperative Sentence + Dependent Temporal Clause
- This sentence commands an action ("turn off the lights") with an implied subject ("you"), specifying a condition ("before you leave"), which sets the timing for the command to be followed.

AI Analysis (NLP):

- **Command Interpretation**: AI identifies "Please turn off" as an imperative command, understanding the polite request for an action to be performed on a specified object ("the lights"). The model leverages patterns from training data to recognize imperative structures, even when the subject is implicit.
- **Temporal Clause Processing**: The use of "before" signals AI to recognize a dependent temporal clause, indicating the condition under which the main action should be carried out. AI understands this clause's role in specifying when the command should be executed, relating it to the sequence of actions.
- **Implied Noun Recognition**: While "you" is the pronoun for the implied subject in the command, AI also infers the presence of an implied noun (the listener or the person being addressed) based on the imperative structure and the context provided by the temporal clause. This ability

to recognize implied subjects and objects showcases AI's nuanced understanding of language beyond explicit textual elements.

Case Study 5: "The lawyer argued the case fiercely in court."

Parts of Speech Breakdown:

- **Determiner**: "The" specifies which lawyer and which case are being discussed.
- **Noun**: "Lawyer" is the subject performing the action; "case" is the object affected by the action.
- **Verb**: "Argued" indicates the action performed by the subject.
- **Adverb**: "Fiercely" modifies the verb, describing the manner of the action.
- **Preposition**: "In" introduces the location of the action.
- **Noun (Location)**: "Court" specifies where the action took place.

Grammar Analysis:

- **Sentence Type**: Simple
- **Structure**: Subject + Verb + Object + Manner + Location
- This sentence describes a straightforward action (argued) carried out by a subject (the lawyer) regarding an object (the case), done in a particular manner (fiercely) and at a specific location (in court).

AI Analysis (NLP):

- **Action and Entity Recognition**: AI identifies "The lawyer" as a Person entity engaging in a specific action ("argued"), and "the case" as an event or legal matter being acted upon. It recognizes "court" as a specific type of Location where legal activities occur.
- **Manner and Location Processing**: Beyond identifying the grammatical structure, AI's NLP capabilities allow it to understand the significance of "fiercely" as indicating the intensity of the lawyer's argumentation style. The inclusion of "in court" is crucial for setting the scene, with AI understanding this as the relevant legal context for the action.
- **Implied Significance**: While all parts of speech are explicitly identified, AI also infers the significant weight and stakes involved in the scenario, considering the legal context and the manner of argumentation. This inference is based on AI's training data, which likely includes information on the typical connotations of arguing a case "fiercely" within a courtroom setting.

Review

Through the detailed exploration presented in these case studies, we've undertaken a comparative journey that highlights both the mechanics of traditional grammatical analysis and the nuanced comprehension of AI through NLP. Each case study served as a microcosm of the broader linguistic landscape, where the foundational elements of sentence structure—parts of speech, syntax, and semantics—are both clearly defined and dynamically interpreted.

The traditional grammar analyses provided a systematic breakdown of sentence components, reinforcing the importance of understanding language at its most elemental level. This approach underscores the value of grammatical literacy in enhancing clarity, precision, and effectiveness in communication. By dissecting sentences into their constituent parts, we gain insight into the intricate rules that govern language structure and the ways in which these rules facilitate coherent expression.

In contrast, the AI analyses, informed by NLP techniques, demonstrated how computational models interpret the same sentences. These models go beyond mere identification of grammatical elements, leveraging vast datasets and algorithms to infer context, intent, and nuanced meaning. The AI's ability to recognize entities, parse dependencies, and understand implied elements within sentences showcases the advanced capabilities of current language technologies. This not only offers a glimpse into how machines process human language but also highlights the potential for AI to assist in linguistic analysis and content creation.

The comparison between traditional and AI-driven analyses reveals a fascinating intersection of human linguistic expertise and machine learning. While traditional analysis provides a solid framework for understanding sentence structure, AI brings a depth of contextual and semantic understanding that can augment human capabilities. However, the AI's interpretations also underscore the technology's limitations, particularly in handling ambiguous or highly nuanced language, reflecting areas where human insight remains indispensable.

In conclusion, these case studies illuminate the complementary strengths of traditional grammatical knowledge and AI-powered language processing. As we continue to advance in both linguistic scholarship and AI development, the synergy between these domains promises to enrich our understanding of language and enhance our ability to communicate effectively. By embracing both perspectives, we can leverage the precision of grammar and the contextual sensitivity of AI to navigate the complexities of language with greater insight and creativity.

Similarities and Differences

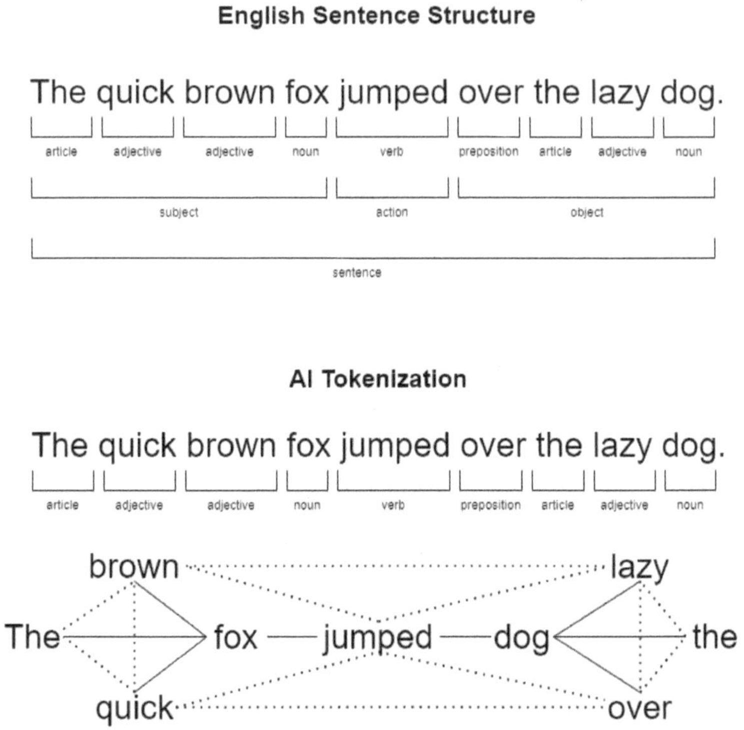

Chart 2, a visual representation of how humans and AI interact with words in a sentence.

The field of Natural Language Processing (NLP) enables AI to parse and interpret human language in ways that mirror certain aspects of traditional grammar understanding. However, there are distinct differences in how AI systems and humans' approach and understand language structures and meanings. This section explores the similarities and differences between AI's understanding of language and human grammar concepts.

Similarities

Foundational Linguistics

At their core, both traditional grammar and AI-driven NLP systems are built upon the bedrock of foundational linguistics, which includes the classification of words into parts of speech, the structure of sentences, and the application of syntactic rules. This shared foundation is pivotal for both approaches to decode the intricacies of language effectively.

- **Parts of Speech**: Identifying nouns, verbs, adjectives, and other parts of speech is a critical first step in both human and AI language understanding. This classification system provides the essential building blocks for constructing sentences and interpreting their meanings. For AI, parts of speech tagging is often the entry point into more complex linguistic analyses, mirroring the way humans first learn to recognize and categorize words based on their functions.
- **Linguistic Rules**: Both methodologies rely on an understanding of linguistic rules to parse sentences accurately. Traditional grammarians have long codified these rules, providing a manual for sentence construction and analysis. AI models, conversely, learn these rules through exposure to vast amounts of text data, internalizing patterns and structures that reflect traditional grammatical principles.

Syntactic and Semantic Processing

Understanding the syntax (sentence structure) and semantics (meaning) of language is crucial for both traditional analysis and AI algorithms. This shared focus allows for the meaningful interpretation of text and the ability to infer context and intent.

- **Syntax Analysis:** The syntactic structure of a sentence—how words and phrases are arranged—plays a critical role in determining its meaning. Both grammarians and AI systems analyze these structures to understand relationships between sentence components. AI uses syntactic parsing to break down sentences into their constituent parts, a process that mirrors human grammatical analysis.
- **Semantic Understanding:** Delving into semantics, both approaches strive to grasp the meanings conveyed by words and phrases within their specific contexts. Humans leverage intuition and experience, while AI models apply sophisticated algorithms to discern patterns and meanings from data. The objective remains the same: to comprehend the intended message and the nuances of language use.

Communication Enhancement

Ultimately, the goal of both traditional grammar and AI's linguistic capabilities is to enhance communication. By ensuring clarity, coherence, and contextually appropriate language use, these approaches facilitate more effective expression and understanding.

- **Clarity and Precision:** Both traditional grammar rules

and AI's language processing aim to improve the clarity and precision of communication. Grammar provides the guidelines for clear expression, while AI offers tools and technologies to assist in achieving this clarity, such as grammar checkers and language generation models.

- **Language Learning and Support:** Traditional grammar education aids language learners in understanding the structure and rules of a language, enhancing their ability to communicate effectively. Similarly, AI-driven language technologies support language learning through personalized tools and resources, offering real-time corrections, suggestions, and language practice opportunities.
- **Adaptive Communication:** Recognizing the dynamic nature of language, both fields emphasize adaptability. Traditional grammar evolves to accommodate new linguistic trends and usage, while AI systems continuously learn from new data to reflect current language practices. This adaptability ensures that both human and machine analyses of language remain relevant and effective.

Differences

Processing Scale and Speed

- **AI's Computational Efficiency**: AI excels in processing vast amounts of text data rapidly, analyzing and interpreting sentences at a scale and speed unattainable for human analysts. This capability enables the handling of large datasets, offering insights and patterns that might be overlooked or take significantly longer to uncover manually.
- **Human Focused Analysis**: While humans cannot match AI's

speed and scale, the depth of understanding in individual or smaller sets of sentences allows for a nuanced interpretation that considers broader contexts and subtleties. Human analysts are adept at providing deep insights on a case-by-case basis, focusing on quality and depth over quantity.

Evolution and Learning

- **AI's Data-Driven Adaptation**: AI systems continuously evolve based on new data, learning from updated information to refine their language models. This data-driven adaptation process allows AI to stay current with linguistic trends and changes, albeit with the caveat of requiring substantial and diverse datasets for retraining.
- **Human Cognitive Flexibility**: Humans adapt to new linguistic information through cognitive flexibility, seamlessly integrating new language use and societal changes without the need for external updates. This innate adaptability enables humans to understand and use emerging language forms intuitively, reflecting a dynamic and responsive approach to linguistic evolution.

Error Correction and Creativity

- **AI's Consistency**: AI tools can provide consistent analysis across large datasets, minimizing human errors that may arise from fatigue or oversight. The uniform application of rules and models ensures a reliable standard of analysis, particularly beneficial for repetitive or formulaic tasks.
- **Human Creativity and Error Handling**: Humans excel at creative language use and can effectively handle ambiguous

or novel expressions that challenge strict grammatical rules. The ability to creatively interpret and produce language, coupled with the capacity to understand and correct errors contextually, showcases the human advantage in adapting language rules and engaging with complex linguistic scenarios creatively.

Summary

Both traditional grammatical analysis and AI's interpretation of sentences offer distinct advantages and face unique constraints. AI's strengths lie in its ability to process language on a large scale efficiently, adapt based on extensive data, and apply consistent analysis across datasets. Conversely, human analysis shines in its depth of understanding, cognitive flexibility in adapting to new language forms, and the capacity for creativity and nuanced error correction. Recognizing these differences without favoring one over the other highlights the complementary potential of integrating human expertise with AI capabilities to achieve a more holistic and effective approach to language understanding.

Insights from AI: Beyond Traditional Grammar Rules

Artificial Intelligence (AI) in Natural Language Processing (NLP) offers unique insights into text analysis that extend beyond the boundaries of traditional grammar rules. These capabilities enable AI to understand and interpret human language in innovative ways, providing valuable perspectives on sentiment, context, and more.

Sentiment Analysis

AI's ability to perform sentiment analysis is a significant leap beyond traditional grammar. This process involves evaluating the emotional tone behind a sequence of words to understand the attitudes, opinions, and emotions expressed by the writer or speaker. For instance, AI can analyze customer reviews to determine whether the feedback is positive, negative, or neutral. This insight is invaluable for businesses to gauge customer satisfaction, for media to understand public sentiment on various issues, and for individuals to filter content based on emotional tone.

Contextual Understanding

AI models, particularly those based on advanced neural networks like transformers, excel at understanding context within a body of text. Unlike traditional grammar, which focuses on the syntactic structure of individual sentences, AI can analyze the broader context across paragraphs or entire documents. This ability allows AI to disambiguate words with multiple meanings, understand idiomatic expressions, and even detect sarcasm or humor, which are often challenging for humans without contextual clues.

Co-reference Resolution

AI's capacity for co-reference resolution enables it to identify when different words or phrases in a text refer to the same entity. For example, in the text "Alice drove her car to the store. She bought milk," AI understands that "She" refers to "Alice" and "her car" refers to "the car" owned by Alice. This insight helps AI maintain consistency in understanding and summarizing long passages of text, a task that requires going beyond sentence-level grammar analysis.

Entity Recognition and Relationship Extraction

Beyond identifying grammatical components, AI can recognize named entities (e.g., people, places, organizations) and extract relationships between them. This capability allows AI to construct knowledge graphs from text, mapping out how different entities are connected. For instance, AI can analyze news articles to identify key figures, organizations, locations, and events, and then map out the relationships between them, offering insights into the underlying structure of information that traditional grammar does not address.

Predictive Text and Language Generation

AI's understanding of language extends to predicting subsequent words in a sentence or generating entirely new text based on a given prompt. This capability, exemplified by models like GPT (Generative Pre-trained Transformer), goes beyond grammar to understand stylistic and thematic elements of language. AI can write stories, compose poetry, or generate informative text, learning from vast datasets to mimic human-like language proficiency.

Conclusion

As we conclude our comparative analysis between AI and traditional grammar, we stand at a fascinating crossroads of language and technology. This exploration has illuminated not only the intricate workings of traditional grammar but also how AI, through its computational lens, interprets and processes the complexities of human language.

Traditional grammar, with its rich history and nuanced understanding of language structure, offers a solid foundation for effective communication. Its principles guide us in crafting sentences that are clear, coherent, and expressive. On the other hand, AI brings a new dimension to language understanding, employing algorithms and vast datasets to parse and generate text in ways that mimic human language processing.

This journey reveals a complementary relationship between human expertise in grammar and AI's capabilities. While AI can handle language at an unprecedented scale, it still grapples with the subtleties of context, nuance, and creative expression that come naturally to humans. Conversely, AI's ability to analyze large volumes of text and identify patterns can enhance our understanding of language and support us in refining our communication skills.

Our comparative analysis underscores the importance of leveraging both traditional grammar and AI to enrich our interactions with language. As AI technology continues to evolve, its integration with traditional linguistic knowledge promises to open new avenues for innovation in communication, education, and beyond.

In essence, the marriage of AI and traditional grammar is not a contest but a collaboration, each bringing its strengths to the table. As we navigate this exciting landscape, we are reminded of the enduring power of language as a tool for expression and connection, and the endless possibilities that lie ahead in understanding and harnessing this power through the lens of AI.

5

Crafting Better Prompts

As we transition into a focused exploration on crafting better AI prompts, it's crucial to reflect on the journey we've embarked upon thus far. Our exploration of traditional grammar and AI's interpretation of sentences has not only illuminated the structural and functional underpinnings of language but also revealed the intricate dance between human linguistic intuition and computational linguistic processing. This rich tapestry of insights forms the foundation upon which we can build more effective, nuanced, and coherent interactions with AI.

Understanding the nuanced differences and surprising parallels between how humans and AI process language is akin to navigating a complex linguistic map. On one hand, traditional grammar offers us the rules and frameworks that have governed human communication for centuries—structures that dictate the flow and form of our sentences. On the other hand, AI, through Natural Language Processing (NLP), interprets and generates language in ways that both mimic and deviate from these established rules. It's this intersection of human linguistic expertise and AI's computational approach that opens up new avenues for enhancing how we communicate with machines.

The ability to craft effective AI prompts is not merely about achieving a functional exchange of information. It's about harnessing the power of language to bridge the gap between human thought and AI comprehension, to translate our queries and commands into a form that AI can process efficiently and accurately. This requires a deep understanding of both the grammatical principles that guide sentence construction and the ways in which AI algorithms interpret these linguistic structures. By applying the lessons learned from our comparative analyses, we are better equipped to formulate prompts that align more closely with AI's interpretative mechanisms, leading to more meaningful and productive outcomes.

As we delve into the nuances of prompt crafting, it's important to remember that this is an evolving art form. Just as language itself is dynamic and ever-changing, so too is the field of AI. The strategies and insights we discuss in this section are grounded in our current understanding of AI capabilities and limitations. However, the landscape of AI is continually advancing, driven by breakthroughs in machine learning, data processing, and computational linguistics. Thus, the journey of refining our communication with AI is ongoing, with each interaction providing an opportunity to learn, adapt, and enhance our approach.

In this section, we will explore in detail how the grammatical insights and AI processing understanding we've acquired can be directly applied to crafting more effective AI prompts. We'll cover key principles for structuring prompts that are clear, concise, and aligned with AI's linguistic capabilities, as well as strategies for incorporating context, managing complexity, and iterating based on feedback. This exploration will not only enhance our immediate interactions with AI but also contribute to the broader dialogue on human-AI communication, paving the way for more intuitive and efficient collaborations between humans and machines in the future.

Leveraging Grammatical Structures

Emphasizing Clarity Through Simple Structures

Given AI's reliance on identifying key components of sentences, such as subjects, verbs, and objects, structuring prompts with clear and simple grammatical constructions can significantly enhance AI's ability to comprehend and respond accurately. Simple sentence structures—subject-verb-object (SVO)—provide a direct pathway for AI to parse the intent of a prompt, ensuring a higher likelihood of a relevant response.

- **Example**: Instead of "Could you provide information on the topic?", use "What is the topic?"

Utilizing Complex Structures for Detailed Queries

While simple structures are effective for straightforward requests, complex sentence structures enable the conveyance of more detailed inquiries or commands. Incorporating dependent clauses, conditional statements, and modifiers can add depth to prompts, allowing for more nuanced interactions with AI. However, it's crucial to balance complexity with clarity to avoid confusing AI models.

- **Example**: "If it's raining, can you suggest indoor activities?" This structure clearly sets a condition that guides the AI's response.

Incorporating Specific Contextual Clues

Context plays a significant role in how AI interprets prompts. By embedding specific contextual clues within grammatical structures, prompts can guide AI towards the intended meaning or domain, enhancing the relevance of its responses. This is particularly important when dealing with topics that require specialized knowledge or when the prompt's context might not be immediately apparent.

- **Example**: "In the context of 19th-century literature, who is the author of 'Pride and Prejudice'?" Here, the prepositional phrase "In the context of 19th-century literature" provides essential context that narrows down the AI's search scope.

Adapting to AI's Interpretative Models

Understanding that AI processes language based on patterns learned from vast datasets can inform how we structure prompts. Phrasing questions or commands in ways that are commonly represented in AI's training data can improve the system's ability to understand and respond to them. This might involve mimicking the phrasing of questions or statements that the AI is likely to have encountered during its training.

- **Example**: Use "Define the term 'photosynthesis'" instead of "I'm wondering what 'photosynthesis' means."

Future Directions

As AI continues to evolve, so will the strategies for crafting effective prompts. The insights gained from leveraging grammatical structures today lay the groundwork for more sophisticated interactions tomorrow. Future explorations will delve deeper into the nuances of human-AI communication, investigating emerging patterns, and innovating new ways to enhance prompt effectiveness. This ongoing journey promises not only to improve our immediate interactions with AI but also to contribute to the broader development of AI's linguistic understanding, opening up new possibilities for collaboration and creativity.

By applying these principles, we harness the power of language to communicate more effectively with AI, creating a bridge between human intent and computational interpretation. This not only enhances the utility and efficiency of AI interactions but also contributes to the continuous improvement of AI's language processing capabilities.

Acknowledging AI's Interpretative Capabilities and Limits

AI's Interpretative Capabilities

- **Pattern Recognition**: AI excels in recognizing patterns within data, including linguistic patterns. This strength allows AI to quickly identify the structure of sentences and the relationships between words based on the vast amount of text it has processed. By crafting prompts that align with recognizable patterns, we can leverage AI's strength in pattern recognition for more accurate responses.

- **Entity Recognition and Categorization**: AI's ability to identify and categorize entities within a sentence is a testament to its advanced NLP capabilities. When constructing prompts, explicitly mentioning key entities (e.g., people, places, concepts) can help AI grasp the context and intent more effectively, leading to responses that are more aligned with the user's expectations.

AI's Interpretative Limitations

- **Understanding Ambiguity and Nuance**: Despite significant advancements, AI still struggles with interpreting ambiguity and nuance in language. Subtle distinctions, implied meanings, and cultural references can sometimes be lost or misunderstood by AI. When creating prompts, it's beneficial to minimize ambiguity and be as explicit as possible about the desired information or action, especially when dealing with complex or nuanced topics.
- **Grasping Context Beyond Immediate Text**: AI's understanding of context is largely confined to the text it is directly analyzing or has been trained on. Its ability to infer broader contextual cues that a human might easily understand from minimal information is limited. Therefore, incorporating sufficient context within prompts—without assuming background knowledge—is crucial for guiding AI towards the intended interpretation.

Navigating AI's Capabilities and Limits in Prompt Crafting

- **Explicitness and Detail**: To accommodate AI's limitations in handling ambiguity, prompts should be explicit and detailed. Clearly specifying the context and including all necessary information within the prompt itself can mitigate misunderstandings and lead to more relevant responses from AI.
- **Adapting Prompt Structure**: Experimenting with the structure of prompts—such as rephrasing questions, adding context, or breaking down complex inquiries into simpler components—can help identify formats that AI handles more effectively. This iterative approach allows users to adapt their communication style to fit AI's processing strengths and weaknesses.

Looking Forward

As AI technology continues to evolve, so will its interpretative capabilities and limitations. Staying informed about the latest developments in AI and NLP will enable users to adjust their strategies for crafting prompts, ensuring effective communication with AI systems. Future explorations will undoubtedly delve deeper into advanced techniques for optimizing prompts, further bridging the gap between human intention and AI comprehension.

Other Ways to Improve Prompts

Beyond leveraging grammatical structures and acknowledging AI's interpretative capabilities and limits, there are additional strategies that can refine and enhance the effectiveness of prompts for AI interactions. While this exploration provides a solid foundation, it's important to note that the art of crafting AI prompts is expansive, with many nuances yet to be explored. Here, we briefly touch upon other avenues for prompt optimization, hinting at a deeper exploration in a forthcoming volume dedicated to mastering prompt crafting.

Contextual Enrichment

Adding context can significantly improve AI's response quality by anchoring its understanding in relevant information. This might involve providing background details, specifying the domain of interest, or clarifying the intent behind the prompt. A well-contextualized prompt guides AI in generating responses that are more aligned with the user's expectations.

Precision and Brevity

While detail is important, conciseness can also play a crucial role in crafting effective prompts. Striking a balance between providing enough context for clarity and keeping the prompt succinct can prevent overwhelming the AI or leading it down irrelevant paths. Precision in language choice ensures that every word contributes to the prompt's intent, enhancing AI's focus on delivering the desired outcome.

Iterative Refinement

Viewing prompt crafting as an iterative process allows for continuous improvement in AI interactions. Based on AI's responses, prompts can be refined and adjusted to better capture the desired information or action. This process of refinement, informed by both successes and misinterpretations, gradually hones the user's ability to communicate effectively with AI.

Exploring Advanced Techniques

As AI technology evolves, so do the strategies for interacting with it. Future volumes will delve into advanced techniques for prompt crafting, exploring innovative approaches that leverage the latest developments in AI and NLP. This exploration will include tips for harnessing AI's full potential, such as using specific phrasing to trigger desired models or functionalities and customizing prompts to individual AI systems' strengths.

Conclusion

The journey to mastering AI prompt crafting is ongoing, with each interaction offering insights into the dynamic interplay between human intent and AI interpretation. The strategies discussed here provide a starting point, but there is much more to explore in the realm of effective communication with AI. A forthcoming volume will expand on these foundational strategies, offering a comprehensive guide to crafting prompts that elicit accurate, relevant, and insightful responses from AI, further enhancing our ability to collaborate with these powerful tools. Stay tuned for this next installment, which promises to unlock new dimensions of AI interaction and creativity.

6

Bridging Insights

Embarking on this exploration of traditional grammar and AI's interpretation of sentences has been a journey through the heart of language, illuminating the intricate ways in which we communicate and how these processes are mirrored—and sometimes challenged—by artificial intelligence. Through detailed case studies, comparative analyses, and practical activities, we've navigated the similarities and differences between human linguistic understanding and AI's computational linguistics, uncovering the depths of grammar's role in shaping clear, effective communication.

This exploration has revealed the foundational structures of language, showcasing the significance of parts of speech, sentence construction, and grammatical rules in crafting meaning. By delving into traditional grammar, we've equipped ourselves with the tools to analyze and understand the complexities of language, laying a solid foundation for more effective communication. Simultaneously, our journey into AI's interpretation of sentences has opened our eyes to the capabilities and limitations of current NLP technologies, offering a glimpse into the future of human-AI interaction.

The comparative analysis between traditional grammar and AI has highlighted the importance of precision, context, and adaptability in crafting prompts that AI can understand and respond to effectively. We've learned that while AI can process language at an unprecedented scale and speed, it often lacks the nuance and intuition that come naturally to human communicators. This understanding prompts us to craft our interactions with AI more thoughtfully, considering both the technological marvels and the challenges that lie within AI's linguistic abilities.

As we conclude this volume, it's clear that the journey doesn't end here. The field of AI and language continues to evolve rapidly, with new advancements and insights emerging regularly. Our exploration has set the stage for a deeper dive into optimizing communication with AI, a topic that will be further explored in a forthcoming volume dedicated to crafting better AI prompts. This next installment promises to build on the foundation laid here, offering advanced strategies and insights to enhance our interactions with AI systems.

In closing, this book has not only expanded our understanding of language and AI but also underscored the importance of effective communication in an increasingly digital world. As we move forward, let us carry with us the lessons learned, the insights gained, and the curiosity that drives us to explore the fascinating intersection of linguistics and artificial intelligence. Together, we stand on the brink of a new era in human-AI collaboration, poised to unlock new possibilities and redefine what it means to communicate in the 21st century.

7

Glossary

Abstract Nouns: Nouns that name qualities, ideas, or states rather than concrete objects.

Action Verbs: Verbs that express physical or mental actions.

Adjectives: Words that describe or modify nouns and pronouns.

Adverbs: Words that modify verbs, adjectives, or other adverbs, providing information about how, when, where, why, or to what extent.

AI (Artificial Intelligence): The simulation of human intelligence processes by machines, especially computer systems.

Ambiguity: The quality of being open to more than one interpretation; vagueness.

Auxiliary Verbs: Verbs used in forming the tenses, moods, and voices of other verbs.

Clauses: Groups of words containing a subject and a predicate; can be independent or dependent.

Co-reference Resolution: The task of determining which words in a sentence refer to the same entity.

Common Nouns: Nouns that name general items or concepts, not specific ones.

Concrete Nouns: Nouns that name physical objects that can be observed through the senses.

Conjunctions: Words that join words, phrases, or clauses together.

Contextual Understanding: The ability to understand the context or surrounding text in which a word or phrase appears.

Demonstrative Adjectives: Adjectives that point out specific items.

Dependency Parsing: A method in syntactic parsing focusing on the dependencies between words.

Descriptive Adjectives: Adjectives that qualify nouns directly.

Direct Object: The object that directly receives the action of the verb.

Entity Recognition: The process of identifying named entities (people, places, organizations) in text.

Grammar: The system and structure of a language, including syntax, morphology, and phonology.

Homonyms and Polysemy: Words that have the same spelling or pronunciation as others but differ in meaning.

Indirect Object: The object that indirectly receives the action of the verb, often indicating to whom or for whom the action is done.

Independent Clauses: Clauses that can stand alone as a sentence, expressing a complete thought.

Interjections: Words or phrases that express emotion or exclamation, often standing apart from the main sentence structure.

Language Generation: The process of using AI to produce text that mimics human language.

Linking Verbs: Verbs that connect the subject of a sentence to a subject complement.

Machine Learning Models: Algorithms that allow computers to learn from and make predictions or decisions based on data.

Manner Adverbs: Adverbs that describe how an action is performed.

Modifiers: Words or phrases that provide additional information about other words in a sentence.

NLP (Natural Language Processing): The branch of AI focused on the interaction between computers and humans through natural language.

Neologisms and Slang: Newly coined words or phrases and informal language.

Neural Networks: Computing systems vaguely inspired by the biological neural networks of animal brains.

Nouns: Words that name people, places, things, or ideas.

Object: The entity that is acted upon by the verb in a sentence.

POS (Part-of-Speech) Tagging: The process of marking up a word in a text as corresponding to a particular part of speech.

Personal Pronouns: Pronouns that refer to specific persons or things.

Place Adverbs: Adverbs that show where an action occurs.

Possessive Pronouns: Pronouns that indicate ownership.

Predicate: The part of a sentence or clause containing a verb and stating something about the subject.

Predictive Text: Text generated by AI based on previous inputs or current typing.

Prepositions: Words that show the relationship between a noun (or pronoun) and other words in a sentence.

Pronouns: Words that replace nouns to avoid repetition.

Quantitative Adjectives: Adjectives that indicate quantity or amount.

Relative Pronouns: Pronouns that introduce relative clauses, connecting them to main clauses.

Relationship Extraction: The process of identifying relationships between entities within text.

Semantic Analysis: The process of understanding the meaning and interpretation of words, phrases, and sentences in context.

Sentiment Analysis: The use of NLP to systematically identify, extract, quantify, and study affective states and subjective information.

Sentence Structure: The way in which sentence elements are arranged to form a sentence.

Subject: The part of a sentence or clause that indicates what it is about or who or what performs the action.

Subordinating Conjunctions: Conjunctions that introduce dependent clauses.

Syntactic Parsing: The process of analyzing sentences' syntax to understand their structure and how components interact.

Time Adverbs: Adverbs that indicate when an action happens.

Tokenization: The process of breaking down a text into individual words or tokens.

Verbs: Words that express actions or states of being.

About the Author

Jeffrey Guntly is a seasoned fiction writer who has ventured into the realm of non-fiction with his latest work, "Anatomy of a Sentence: Bridging AI and English Grammar." With a diverse background spanning personal finance and a deep-seated passion for storytelling, Jeffrey brings a unique perspective to the exploration of language and technology.

This book marks Jeffrey's first foray into non-fiction, born out of a fascination with generative AI and a desire to understand and harness its potential responsibly. His journey into writing about AI was sparked by a realization: his proficiency in crafting sentences and engaging narratives significantly enhanced his ability to interact with AI, enabling him to generate better prompts and achieve more meaningful results than many of his peers.

Jeffrey's interests are broad, encompassing not just technology and AI but also consumer electronics, video games, and coffee—a reflection of his curiosity and enthusiasm for exploring new territories. "Anatomy of a Sentence" represents a synthesis of these passions, offering readers insights into the intersection of traditional grammar and cutting-edge AI applications.

Through this book, Jeffrey aims to bridge the gap between the technical world of AI and the creative craft of writing, shedding light on how understanding sentence construction can empower individuals to engage more effectively with artificial intelligence. His hope is that readers will come away with a deeper appreciation for the nuances of language, armed with the knowledge to navigate the evolving landscape of AI-enhanced communication.

You can connect with me on:

- https://www.linkedin.com/in/jeffrey-burros
- https://www.threads.net/@jeffreyguntly

Made in United States
Troutdale, OR
11/03/2026

56844420R00046